Watching the Weather

Sunshine

Elizabeth Miles

Heinemann
LIBRARY

www.heinemann.co.uk/library

To order:
 Phone 44 (0) 1865 888066
Send a fax to 44 (0) 1865 314091
Visit the Heinemann Bookshop at www.heinemann.co.uk/library to browse our catalogue and order online.

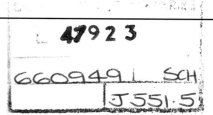
First published in Great Britain by Heinemann Library, Halley Court, Jordan Hill, Oxford OX2 8EJ, part of Harcourt Education.
Heinemann is a registered trademark of Harcourt Education Ltd.

Editorial: Nicole Irving and Tanvi Rai
Design: Richard Parker and Celia Jones
Illustrations: Jeff Edwards
Picture Research: Rebecca Sodergren and Mica Brancic
Production: Séverine Ribierre

Originated by Dot Gradations Ltd.
Printed and bound in China by South China Printing Company

ISBN 0 431 19025 9
09 08 07 06 05
10 9 8 7 6 5 4 3 2 1

British Library Cataloguing in Publication Data
Miles, Elizabeth
  Sunshine. – (Watching the weather)
  551.5'271
A full catalogue record for this book is available from the British Library.

Acknowledgements

The Publishers would like to thank the following for permission to reproduce photographs: Alamy Images pp. 13, 23; Corbis/Clem Haagner/Gallo Images p. 18; Corbis/Craig Tuttle p. 20; Corbis/Norbert Schaefer p. 26; Corbis/Owen Franken p. 14; Corbis/Penny Tweedie p. 25; Corbis/RF pp. 12, 15, 22, 17; Corbis/Viviane Moos p. 24; Eye Ubiquitous/NASA p. 7; Getty/Image Bank p. 5; Getty Images/PhotoDisc pp. i, 10, 16; Harcourt Education Ltd/Trevor Clifford p. 8; Harcourt Education Ltd/Tudor photography pp. 28, 29; OSF/Eyal Bartov p. 19; Robert Harding Picture Library p. 4.

Cover photograph of sunshine streaming through a forest reproduced with permission of Getty Images/Digital Vision.

The Publishers would like to thank Daniel Ogden for his assistance in the preparation of this book.

Every effort has been made to contact copyright holders of any material reproduced in this book. Any omissions will be rectified in subsequent printings if notice is given to the Publishers.

The paper used to print this book comes from sustainable resources.

Contents

Any words appearing in the text in bold, **like this**, are explained in the Glossary.

 Find out more about sunshine at www.heinemannexplore.co.uk

What is sunshine?

Sunshine is light that is given out by the Sun. Some heat comes with the light too. We get sunshine during the daytime. It makes us feel warm on sunny days.

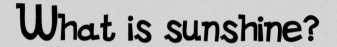

The Sun is a ball of **gas** in space. It is often hidden from us by clouds.

Never look at the Sun, even through sunglasses. Its light can hurt your eyes.

The Sun is a star. It is like the stars we can see in the night sky. The Sun looks much bigger though, because it is the nearest star to us.

The Earth and the Sun

The Earth travels around the Sun in a path called an orbit. As the Earth moves around the Sun, the Earth also spins, or **rotates**.

We cannot feel the Earth moving, but it is moving and spinning all the time.

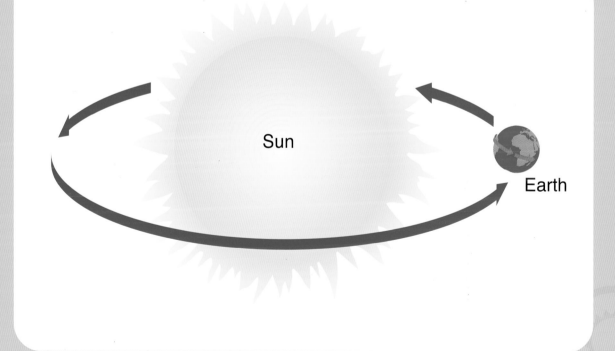

Sun

Earth

As the Earth spins, the Sun's light shines first on one half of the Earth, then the other. This gives us daytime and night-time.

On the bright side of the Earth it is daytime. On the dark side of the Earth it is night-time.

Measuring the Sun's warmth

Sunshine affects how hot or cold the air feels. We call this the air **temperature**. By looking at a thermometer we can see how the air temperature changes.

The higher the red line on a thermometer, the higher the temperature.

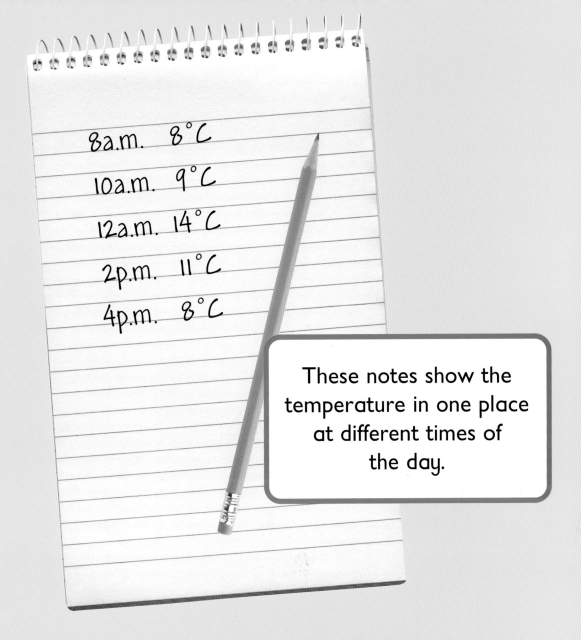

8a.m. 8°C
10a.m. 9°C
12a.m. 14°C
2p.m. 11°C
4p.m. 8°C

These notes show the temperature in one place at different times of the day.

The temperature changes during the day. Often, it starts cool, then gets warmer by midday. In the evening, it gets cooler again.

Sunshine and the seasons

On this sunny winter's day, the sunshine is not hot enough to melt the snow.

In summer we get more of the Sun's heat than in winter. Summer sunshine is warmer. This is because the Earth tilts (leans) as it moves around the Sun.

The Earth's tilt makes part of it lean towards the Sun and part of it lean away. Places tilted towards the Sun get more of the Sun's warmth.

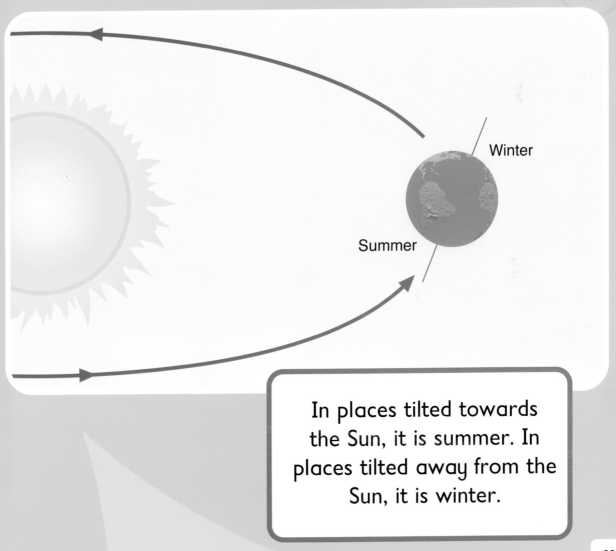

Winter

Summer

In places tilted towards the Sun, it is summer. In places tilted away from the Sun, it is winter.

Heat from the Sun

The Sun's heat feels strongest at the **Equator**. On and near the Equator, you find the hottest places on Earth.

Hot **deserts** have very hot sunshine and very little rain.

The Sun's heat feels weakest at the **Poles**. The Poles are the coldest places on Earth. The sunshine never feels hot here.

At the Poles people have to wear very thick clothes to stay warm.

Sunshine and people

Light-coloured clothes feel cooler than dark-coloured clothes. Light colours **reflect** more of the sunshine away.

Sunshine can burn our skin. It is important to wear a long-sleeved shirt, a hat and suncream on sunny days. In hot **deserts** people often wear light-coloured clothes.

Light from the Sun can damage our eyes. Snow reflects the light up into our eyes. This makes the sunlight even more dangerous.

Skiers wear sunglasses to protect their eyes from the light. Suncream protects their skin from sunburn.

15

Using sunshine

Some food plants, such as wheat, must dry in warm sunshine before they are ready to be picked.

People make use of the Sun's heat in lots of different ways. Sunshine dries wet clothes on washing lines. Farmers need the Sun to help their plants to grow.

The light and heat from the Sun are a useful kind of **energy**. This energy is called solar power. People use it to make **electricity**.

These panels collect the Sun's light to make electricity. The electricity helps to heat and light our schools and homes.

Sunshine and animals

Some animals, such as crocodiles, need the Sun's heat to warm their bodies. Other animals make their own **energy** to keep them warm.

Crocodiles lie in the sunshine on riverbanks to warm up and get their bodies moving.

It is dangerous for many animals to get too hot in the Sun. Some animals lie in the shade or wade in rivers to cool down.

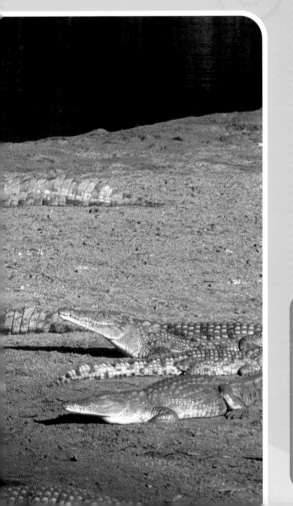

This fox lives in a hot **desert**. It digs a tunnel in the sand and hides from the hot sunshine in the daytime.

Sunshine and plants

Green plants need sunshine to make their food. Plants take in some of the sunshine in their leaves. They use it to make food from air and water.

Plants die without sunshine because they cannot make their food.

Plants cannot live and grow without sunshine. If there were no plants, animals would die too. Animals and people would have nothing to eat.

Plants, animals and people need sunshine to live.

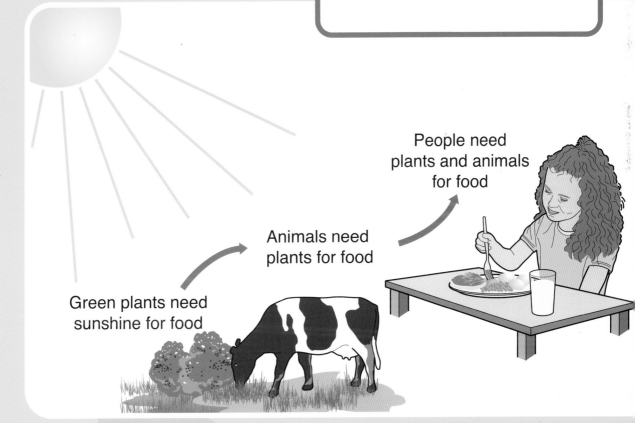

People need plants and animals for food

Animals need plants for food

Green plants need sunshine for food

Sunshine and drought

A drought is when a place does not get enough rain for a long time. Hot sunshine can dry up any water that is left in the ground.

During a drought, the ground can quickly dry up and form cracks.

Many plants die in a drought. Without grass or other plants to eat, animals die too. People may starve if there is nothing left to eat.

Under the hot sunshine and without any water, farmers' food plants die.

Disaster: heatwave

A heatwave is when summer sunshine is hotter than usual. People find it hard to work. Some people suffer from sunstroke, an illness caused by too much sunshine.

It can be hard to cool down during a heatwave.

If there has been no rain, plants and trees dry up in the Sun. Dry plants burn easily.

During heatwaves, huge fires sometimes sweep through forests and fields. If there are hot, dry winds, the fires spread very quickly.

Warmer weather

When people burn **fuels**, **waste gases** rise into the air. These **gases** can make the Earth warmer than normal. This is called global warming.

Fuel is burned in factories and in homes. The waste gases can make the Earth warmer.

Waste gases hang in the air around the Earth. After the Sun has warmed the Earth, this heat usually rises back up. The waste gases can trap this heat nearer the ground, making the Earth warmer.

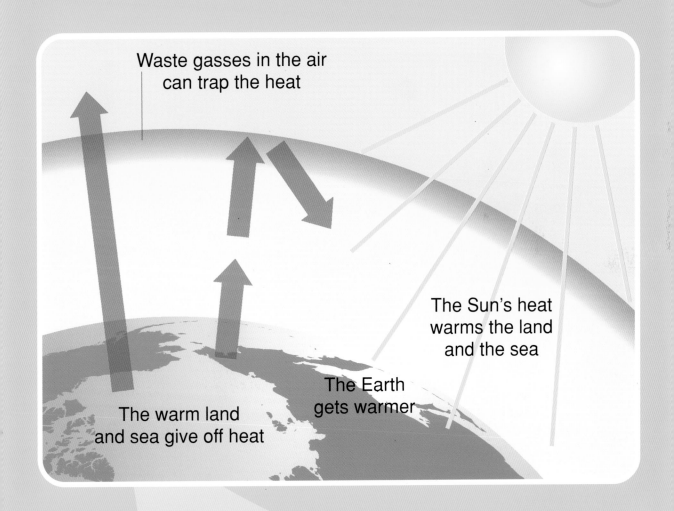

Waste gasses in the air can trap the heat

The Sun's heat warms the land and the sea

The Earth gets warmer

The warm land and sea give off heat

Project: sunshine and water

Find out how powerful sunshine can be. See how quickly its heat makes water turn into a **gas** called **water vapour**.

1. On a hot, sunny day fill the saucer almost to the top with water.

2. Draw a line on the saucer at the edge of the water.

3. Put the saucer in a sunny place.

4. Every 2 hours mark the edge of the water again. How quickly does the water go down?

5. Try the experiment again on a cool, cloudy day. How quickly does the water go down this time?

What happens?
The water in the saucer goes down because the Sun's heat turns some of it into a gas that goes into the air. The way it does this is called **evaporation**.

 Find out more about sunshine at www.heinemannexplore.co.uk

29

Glossary

desert place with very little rain. Some deserts are hot and some deserts are cold.

electricity type of energy that makes lots of things work, such as lights and computers

energy power that makes things work. Heat and light are kinds of energy.

Equator imaginary line round the centre of the Earth

evaporation how water changes from a liquid to a gas that you cannot see

fuel things like wood or petrol that are burned to make energy

gas something you cannot hold or pour. Air is a gas.

Poles the North and South Poles are the two points furthest from the Equator. They are the coldest places on Earth.

reflects sends back. A mirror reflects a picture of your face when you look in it.

rotates spins round and round

temperature measure of how hot or cold something is

waste gases dirty air that comes out when fuels are burned

water vapour water that is part of the air. Water vapour is a gas that we cannot see.

Find out more

More books to read

What is Weather? Sunshine, Miranda Ashwell and Andy Owen (Heinemann Library, 1999)

Geography Starts Here! Weather Around You, Angela Royston (Hodder Wayland, 2001)

What is Weather? Watching the Weather, Miranda Ashwell and Andy Owen (Heinemann Library, 1999)

Websites to visit

http://www.weatherwizkids.com
A website packed with information about weather features, satellite images from space, games and fun activities to do with the weather.

http://www.planetpals.com/weather.html
Learn more about different sorts of weather and interesting weather facts to share with friends.

Index

Titles in the *Watching the Weather* series include:

Hardback   0 431 19022 4

Hardback   0 431 19023 2

Hardback   0 431 19024 0

Hardback   0 431 19025 9

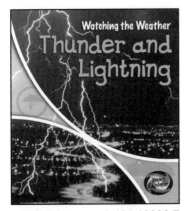

Hardback   0 431 19026 7

Find out about the other titles in this series on our website www.heinemann.co.uk/library